Love Notes From, Sophia

A Journey of Awakening, Remembering, Release & Rebirth

SOPHIA RENEE

Love Notes From, Sophia
Copyright © 2022

ALL RIGHTS RESERVED

No part of this book may be reproduced or transmitted in any form or by any means without the written consent of the author or publisher.

Publisher: AmaZen by Design LLC, Lawrenceville, GA 30045

Format: Hardcover
Written and designed by: Sophia Renee
Available from: Amazon
ISBN 979-884251223-2

DEDICATION

To My Duckies.
My then, now, and forever.

ACKNOWLEDGEMENTS

To Clara, the woman who raised me, for being a role model as a prayer warrior and for being the love in the house amidst chaos and dysfunction.

To Grandma Clemmie, the strength of a woman that raised generations. Thank you for spaghetti dinners on bamboo plate holders.

To Mama "B" for loving me and grafting me into your spiritual and natural family.

To Earnestine, aka "Tina", for the woman I am becoming. Thank you for risking being called an even more weird hippy and reading to your belly in 1969.

To Dana, Mi Padrino Blanco Especial. I will always love you.

To Frank Crimbley. Thank you for love, laughter, family, and my nose.

To my spiritual teachers and guides: Gratitude for your service, knowledge, wisdom, patience, and Love.

To all my lovers and muses: If you have ever inspired me to write, you were lighting the way for angels to dance in the darkest corners of my soul.

Table of Contents

DEDICATION 3
ACKNOWLEDGEMENTS 4
   Foreword by Shura Muhummed 6

JOURNEY TO SOPHIA, PART I 12
Life, Love and Spirit 12

   Soul Fishing 16
   Truth 16
   Channeling 17
   Third Eye 17
   Sine Waves and Asymptotes 18
   Sunrise 23
   Skin 24
   Miss Celie's Blues (The Remix) 27
   Spent 28
   Cathartic Confessions 30
   Narcissist 30
   Letting It Flow 31
   Plugged Tears 33
   Myspace and White Chocolate 35
   Limits (For Baseball Man) 38
   Home 39

The Cycle of Letting Go..40

Katrina..41

Soul Ties..42

ALPJTJ...44

I, Since You 45

Love Is a Flower 46

JOURNEY TO SOPHIA, PART II 48
Spirituality, Sexuality & Erotica 48

Go Within 54

Cocoon...55

Lost...58

Grow In Grace 61

Letter to Little Sophia..62

You Won't Lose 64

Spiritual Midwives 65

Waking Up 67

Doing The Work...67

Bars From the Matrix 68

Growth (Haiku)...68

Present 69

You Got This 69

Fall 70

Heart Poetry 71

Manifesto	72
Stirring	73
Awakening (Ode to John)	74
Naked	75
A Drop of Water	76
Archaeology	77
Hello, Sir. Render	78
528 Hertz	80
Kintsukuroi	80
Titillation	80
Marinate	81
Hearts Open	82
Torque	82
The Awakening of Sophia	83
Shavasana	84
Grapes and Shit	86
Lotus Flower	90
More Please	92
Those Hands	93
QOTD	94
Heart Sex	95
Oral Surgery	96
Bedtime	97
Welcome Home	98

Longing 100
Sticky 101
Mix? 102
Tantric Love: An Erotic Short Story 106
JOURNEY TO SOPHIA CONTINUES 113
A Peek into My Chrysalis 113
About the Author 114

LOVE NOTES FROM, SOPHIA

Foreword
By Shura Muhummed

DO you believe that God works through people?

When I first laid eyes on Sophia Renee, I was moved and impressed by her child-widened eyes, the sister ship of the 'full-lipped', and her womaned audacity. We met in a Facebook group, one full of spiritually inquisitive expatriates who were questioning our investment in societal constructs and mindsets that had been normalized but had not experienced a *rebirth*. The outlying nature of the many groups evolved from hearts chopping at the bit, in want of something more. These portals were sometimes flighty and unpredictable, but they became the genesis of some of the most stimulating conversations and studies we see highlighted in 2022. They held wonders and revelations that we thirsted for. Little did I know that having a friend like Sophia would give me a front seat to what painted vibrant animation of the spirit and the beauty of sacred exploration and celebration would look like.

As a child of the '70s, Sophia is the personification of great reverential practices and the simultaneous interrogation of the orthodox. Her piece, "The Lotus Flower" spoken six years ago directly addressed this entanglement. In this heartfelt testimony, *Love Notes From Sophia*, you get dipped in the sauce and pulled onto the dance floor that reverberates with ancestral Tambor drumbeats that'll lick you with fire. From then to now, her writings, inquiries, and healing quests continue to erase lines and bring courage and the cataclysmic into view.

Her prior works roil with authentic cadence and rhythmic phrases that make inroads, ever so gingerly, peppering your heart as she holds your hand. She's a good friend like that. Her continuous rebirths take you into her inner sanctum brushing you up against your inner revolutionary who might not quite be ready to leap but who remains intrigued just enough to travel down the yellow brick road.

It was early 2015, both of us young mothers, amid the upheaval and holy transmutation that created a knowingness, a sisterhood, a bridge, a familiarity. The seamlessness of our connection felt ancient. Since then, we've crisscrossed, seeking guidance, virtual hugs, and spiritual caretaking.

As the years passed, I saw flashes of that tenacious eastside Tallahassee zing become emboldened to challenge directives, change directions, make supreme sacrifices, pick up, pack up, and carry on to a more promising land. Her motivation has matured and comes in the faces of her three children – the desire for the greater, more evolved, and open-minded has set their lives on a course that has become a wellspring of lessons. Sophia is earning her full lotus by penetrating her heart, the mysterious, and diving into the ocean of life to not only be at peace but also be fully present.

As years passed, I supplemented naivete and my sheltered living by riding shotgun with this 'Goddess general' who knew how to use kid gloves to inquire and elicit answers using her sagacious chisel with the lightened tip so you could peek inside and see what was about to be dispelled, deliberated, or destroyed.

Whether it be in Sophia's 'journeyed' writings, healing modalities, or random videos – the same intention was clear; whatever was pressing was about to be cleaned up or cleaned out —even if it meant that Sophia was placing herself squarely underneath the microscope herself.

The truth of, *As Above, So Below* was her mantra that promoted a heart-centered coherence furthered by her unfoldment into a humbled surrender.

Our Facebook forays took us in and out of one another's space, but not out of one another's life – she might not know until reading this that she became a muse for me. Her movements, energetically expressed and dynamically felt, inspired me to push on in my voyage. I was so wetted behind the ears and full of fears and scars, but intermittently I could sync up with the discoveries that she had dared to take on. I was in awe of her kindness even when saturated by the storms.

She may have wanted things to be easy, but she wasn't afraid to do the hard. It had to be the furnace of that fire starter Aries that gilded her. It all became strangely familiar to me because her nature was like my then partner – and as a water sign, I was being transported and transformed by their passions and leadership. I was impressed by their ways.

And isn't that what it takes, us facing ourselves and taking that mustard seed of courage to be the leader in our living so that our path can be unshackled and forged. If you need a blueprint, peruse these pages where evidence of Sophia being shaken, stirred, sifted, and shifted by curiosity burns holes until it gets to the Truth of the matter.

You may think that with this cherished intimacy I speak of that I have met my darling Sophia in person. I have not. What this so eloquently demonstrates is the power and impact we can have upon one another. We are all divine energetic limitless beings. The influence of our reach is not something to take lightly. From the words we speak to the actions and intentions we place into the Universe – it all is a ripple in the ocean of our Oneness.

My life is forever changed by having the experience of knowing Sophia Renee. I hope that you will partake in the linguistic jewelry she is offering you. She is lovingly asking you to consider and potentially adorn yourself as you walk out the supernatural synergy of your own light. Take notes, catch your breath, and be informed by the holy instrumentation of a soul on fire. Sophia is treating us to her work of heart.

May the soulful investigative reporting done here by way of tears, heartache, pleasure, recalibration, and rebirth bless your spirit and your shelves.

Come to the table and welcome to the feast of *Love Notes From, Sophia.*

You will not leave the same, you may become so full that you experience your own REBIRTH.

LOVE NOTES FROM, SOPHIA

JOURNEY TO SOPHIA, PART I
Life, Love and Spirit

When I got "saved" for real, they taught us about going into our prayer (secret) closet. I took that teaching literally and I used to go into my narrow, walk-in closet that had a chair in the back. Daily, I would kneel and talk to God. I would talk to God throughout my day. I was a self-initiated student of the Bible and developed a practice of prayer and fasting. I experienced God in that closet.

I experienced God (Love) during a church service after the death of my grandfather and my heart was completely shut down with no desire or care about living – complete apathy. God poured his Spirit down, wrapped me up in a blanket of Love and cracked my heart wide open while I was standing (hiding) on the back pew.

I experienced holy laughter during a church service and cried tears. I was releasing the weight, sadness, and bittersweet grief of my grandfather's death, after years of verbal, sexual, and physical abuse.

I experienced God with lovers in the bedroom, feeling energy move through my entire body and blow straight through my crown. I spoke in tongues the same way I did my first time at the altar in church while seeking to be filled with the Holy Ghost.

I experienced God in the middle of a tantric healing demonstration, crying tears and speaking in tongues, while the "goddess" activated the Kundalini energy in a male volunteer.

I experienced God in an ayahuasca ceremony when my heart was flooded so much with love that my insides felt like they would burst. I had a cheesy grin on my face like Celie from *The Color Purple*.

I have experienced whom I call God in many different experiences, channels, and spaces. I don't know why people need to call God a certain name or experience God in a certain context to accept who or *that* God is. I may have a new experience tomorrow and I'm open to that.

My entire life has taken the direction of God-seeker. More recently, I have come to know the God in me. That God-is (Goddess) me. After much disappointment, and the realization that me looking for God outside of myself was the root of my unrealistic expectations and subsequent disillusionment, I decided that I had to stop working so hard to fit into the *god-box* that I allowed others to create for me.

SOPHIA RENEE

    Since God is Love, I accept the truth of who I am created to be: Love.

    The whole world needs more Love.

I Am,

Sophia Renee

LOVE NOTES FROM, SOPHIA

SOPHIA RENEE

Soul Fishing

I went soul fishing today.
What's behind door number three?

Puzzle pieces strewn.
Distractions from me.

It's getting so dark.
Closing my eyes to see.

Taking the labyrinth route
to unlock the mystery.

Truth

The truth is,
I cannot hide from the truth
no matter how much I try
or want to,
or think I need to.
Truth is always there by my side.
And the quality of my life is always
dependent upon my relationship with it.

Channeling

I am a divine distiller of truth.
A sacred farmer tilling the soil of your soul,
infusing your life with sunlight, wind, and rain.
I call you by name.
A name that cannot be written,
but is spoken with the arch of her back
while bloodied, cotton-filled hands fill sacks.
When her hips attempt to brace against
his thrusts of lust and domination,
to dismantle and disturb the course
of legacies and nations
in her womb.
Yet, as the sparrow greets the new moon with her song,
a conscious eruption ensues.

Third Eye

Trust your knowing.
In the stillness, it is growing.
Life's lessons, it is showing.
Power from on high is flowing.
You are growing.
Into a beautiful creation of God's love.

Sine Waves and Asymptotes

Many of my close friends and family would describe me as pensive, reflective, meditative, introspective, *in the clouds* and dreamy. Many have given me the nickname of "Squirrel", and one friend decided that enforcing an imaginary talking stick would be helpful in her attempts to keep me from rambling down a rabbit hole of endless thought!

Much of my thinking is driven by my constant evaluation of whether life was supposed to happen a certain way, and, more importantly, did I respond to life as I should. Constant statistical consideration of permutations, probabilities, outcomes, and the muck in between. After all, my mind can hold a herd of pink elephants, including the spare room in the basement! It feels like I am uniquely gifted at thinking about thoughts and reflecting about reflections:

1. Nowadays, my life seems to require more than the usual fare.
2. The stench of my own egotistic satisfaction from extensive spiritual and intellectual masturbation has been haunting me for weeks!
3. My heart is compelled to convince my mind that every faulty landing and decision was not necessarily wrong, and it certainly does not mean that something *is wrong* with me.

4. There are indeed pockets of truth, bliss, love, redemption, healing, and empowerment that have flavored my journey. However, I spend a lot of time thinking about the past rather than focusing on the present, and my mind gets lost in any attempt to connect the dots.

My writing shows it! *Food for thought on gaining a better understanding of the layers of me.* But that's not what this is about.

My focus is primarily on what *growth* looks like for me. What my evolution, which at times presents like an unannounced revolution. How do we make sense of our spiritual landscape considering the very real and sometimes treacherous terrain that we experience along the way?

I had a conversation with a very dear sister-friend because I was feeling very detached and tentative. Almost as if I were a candle and my life could be blown away with only a whisper. She felt my pain and frustration that my growth and life path was feeling like I had two left feet trying to dance the cha-cha. There was more stepping back and sideways than to the beat and in harmony with my life partner, myself. She replied, "Growth is a constant, inevitable process. The direction, however, is a variation of sine waves and asymptotes." She described my world exactly as I was feeling it in that moment!

I thought someone was playing a trick on me because it felt like I had been searching for truth, coming intimately close to what I thought were answers, but never reaching it. And, feeling like, I never would.

"Growth is a constant, inevitable process. The direction, however, is a variation of sine waves and asymptotes."
~S. D.

It *is* a journey. A pilgrimage! A constant unraveling and unfolding of my personal onion. There were times when I felt like I was losing my grip on what *is*.

Was I really in the Matrix? Had Morpheus unplugged me, and I was in the throes of being flushed down the metaphysical toilet? If so, it felt like a long way down and I had gotten stuck, hoping to feel the push of my spiritual plunger that would propel me into the love and light and the bliss that I had come to experience in the last couple of years of devoting myself to meditation. What I did not fully comprehend was that a spiritual journey is lifelong and all-terrain. It is not the result of mixing alkaline water with a packet of magical dust sprinkled over my life by a shaman because I did the right thing by taking enough classes and attending enough retreats.

Somewhere in my mind(ego), I expected to *arrive* and, aside from a few hiccups, enjoy the constant flow of orgasmic bliss on my way to saving the world. I had developed a vision of sage and incense and beaded curtains, communal living off the grid, and breaking free from the "corporate plantation". How could I know that I was still pulling back layers of programming, belief systems, and the trauma I had collected and rehashed in my 46 years of living? I learned from my meditation teacher, a great servant, that it takes time—a commitment to see it through.

There is no going back. Well, I could go back, but I know where all those roads lead. *Cue the matrix scene where Neo wants to get out of the deal that he had just cemented by taking the red pill, and Trinity describes, with conviction, that he's been there before and needs to get his ass back in the car to see where the rabbit hole leads.* I was tired of the record skipping at that same old spot. But I didn't know how to get unstuck.

I see myself as always having been a spiritual seeker. Growing up in the Baptist church, I got *saved for real* my senior year in high school on a Sunday at a Pentecostal church. The Church of God in Christ (COGIC), to be exact was the greatest expression of God living through his people that I had ever known. I may lose some readers, but I am not stuck on God's gender anymore. I use the terms "He" and "His" as a general and reverent context. To me, God looks like whatever reflection one sees based on where he exists culturally. In the

COGIC church, I had shifted from routine, dogmatic religion to a deep desire to know God for myself. In the beginning, it was their demonstration of love for all people and authentic devotion to the lifestyle that made me want to be like them. I prayed, studied, and memorized scriptures, and fasted so much that I fell unconscious and woke up at the bottom of the stairs one Saturday afternoon. I felt God's spirit visit me three nights in a row but was too afraid to wake up and answer The Call. That same spirit would fall during collegiate choir rehearsals and leave folks drunk and slain in the spirit, weeping, worshiping, and praising God, and giving their lives to Jesus. But unfortunately, I began to focus more on the people instead of God's truth and love and felt like their lives didn't match the words that we sang about on Sunday morning. Of course, I had experienced my falling away, but I truly wanted to be a Christian in my heart. I eventually left the church and didn't want to hear a scripture or anything that resembled *church folk*. What I didn't realize was, that it was a journey. It still is and will continue to be.

Sunrise

In the still of the morning,
I watched the sun rise gently,
like hope peering over the horizon.

And the birds played an intro
as it pushed away the darkness,
lighting up my corner of the world.

Destiny stretched itself over a purple haze.
Opportunity was beaming so loud,
I could hear it say, "Hello, World!"

I said "hello" back and smiled,
lighting up my corner of the world

So, I rose to live again
with hope, destiny, and opportunity in my pouch.

Maybe I'll go cloud surfing today,
lighting up my corner of the world.

SOPHIA RENEE

Skin

Sometimes a prison; sometimes a shelter.
My skin tells a story of how life is.
Resilient, tough, and thick to protect,
stretching when pressed to go beyond the limit,
scarred when the pressure is too hard, too fast.
How delicate when a baby bursts into existence,
totally vulnerable to the elements,
but only by exposure will he grow.

My skin has become a prison of past failures,
hurts, disappointments, and bitterness.
It has hardened over the years
and become scaly and crusty.
Fearful of peeling away to let in.
Nothing escapes.
So, I fester and boil.
Don't press too hard.
The poison will ooze
and infect,
creating the same effect,
for it is contagious.

Destined to live in this shell with no escape,
or so it seems,
my prison becomes a shelter,
in some bizarre way.

Deeply encased below
layers of dead stuff,
screaming for the breath
of life.
I am coiled inside of myself.
I will hurt no more.
I will feel no more.

Can you see through my skin?
Each day I add different layers
to suit the situation.
And it all melds,
until I don't know which is mine,
and which is what you want to see.

Longing for metamorphosis,
as a caterpillar to a butterfly.
Let me sleep and wake up,
a beautifully free person.

Dear God,
send a healing balm
to soften and soothe
the encrusted skin of Life,
slough away the dead weight.
My skin is pulling me down.
I want to fly,
but I am too angry to trust the wind,

SOPHIA RENEE

       too afraid to feel the pang
       of crashing to the ground,
              again.

LOVE NOTES FROM, SOPHIA

Miss Celie's Blues (The Remix)

Swimming against my flow,
I press toward a mark that is not mine to attain.

Married to anxiety; push, pull; push-pull; hurry up and wait.
Constant river of sadness flowing through my valleys.

I am the tree that is falling, and no one will hear.
How long before the waters push the last gasp of air from my lungs?

I feel him calling, but the water's lullaby has drowned my senses, like the fish who needs no eyes in a deep, dark sea.

Tears distilled in a basin of angst.
Who do these motherfuckers think they are messing with?

I swing, but my arms do not move.
Paralysis by analysis.

Had a talk with him last night,
Celie scratched it out of my head today.

I've decided I'm not going down without a fight.

SOPHIA RENEE

Spent

It's been two weeks since I heard his voice.
I was feeling like a penny waiting for change. Spent.
Lamenting in my mind about
how many times
I had visited this familiar, yet empty place.

I brought up the *R* word
and he told me he liked it the way it was.
So, that night, I gave him some extra good head.
And I swallowed.
I thought if I asked for more,
there would be no more.
And with a grip on my heart,
he would walk out the door.

I even chopped, peeled, mixed, fried, baked, and boiled him a
home-cooked meal.
You know, every man needs some greens in his life.
What I didn't realize was that I couldn't sell to someone else
something that I did not respect and value: Myself.

Pressing him to see the queen I could be
but living like a woman,
phenomenally...perpetually...cyclically...in neutral.
Struggling to shift from the world of a broken destiny

LOVE NOTES FROM, SOPHIA

into a place of love and purpose.
Radiating the best of me.
Only he could tell, by my inconsistency,
that the one whom I needed to love the most,
was me!

I had let go of my Father's hand,
trying to follow the *grown 'n sexy* plan.
Disconnected from my Source.
Another love fantasy became a corpse,
when I realized that I was nothing more to him
than the person he met in the parking lot at 2:04 a.m.

And, having tasted my wine
stimulated my mind,
fingertips crawling up and down my spine,
sending pleasure pulses through my spot,
from the bottom to the top,
until I lost all sense of space and time:
he kindly excused himself from the table Divine and said,
"No thanks. I'm full."

SOPHIA RENEE

Cathartic Confessions

My *sorry* feels like a dollar in Germany.
What offering to place on your altar
to express that I was just a scared little girl?
Lost and tormented by the idea that
Cookies need love like everything does.
I crumble at the thought of you.
Seeing my naked body ain't the thing.
but tender thoughts and feelings.
Fear you would see me and my pain,
only to refrain from taking a closer look,
to run your fingers through my book of pearls and poison.

Narcissist

I just wanted to breathe with you.
Be free with you.
Eyes wide shut and see with you.
But you are sucking me dry,
cutting off my high supply
and killing my buzz.
Pulled off my shirt to cover your back
and I'm wandering naked in the forest
to gather more wood,
to stoke your fire,
and keep you warm.

Letting It Flow

So, I write.
Grabbing the pen instead of the knife.
Stroking away the pain and strife.
Feeling like I've lived this life.
Before.
Before it was different.
Or was it the same game that is my claim to fame?
I blame me.
Me for hoping the lie would live another day.
Stay and lay like broccoli.
Tell me you love me and shove reality
far away.
I'll open my eyes another day.

Swoosh, the ink flows across my pages.
This play has been running for ages.
The only things changing are the stages.
And what are my wages?
Time and a half of my heart's rages.
Out of control.
This shit is getting old.
God told me what to do.
Help me to trust in you.
You said it's not over.
But I just keep getting older.

SOPHIA RENEE

I want to be a boulder.
But I'm all gushy inside.
Getting dizzy from this ride.
The not-so-merry-go-round
in circles.

Waves rush in and they cover me.
More like smother me.
And I lose my way.

How will I show the duckies the way?
He walked out of my life yesterday.
Fantasia on replay.

I juiced today and felt good about me.
Me who is the blade of grass peeking through the concrete.
I'm on the cusp.
'B' likes that word.
But I must remove the disgust of my own lust
and embrace all of me.
Destiny. Nice name for a baby girl.
She's going somewhere.
She's got a map, too!
Can you tell me how to get to Sesame Street?
Wish I could be Oscar the Grouch for a day.
Fell asleep on the couch.
In my defense, it was the recliner.

Plugged Tears

An attack of the heart,
waiting for the next beat.
Heavy, piercing, throbbing.
It hurts so bad.
He loves me?
He loves me not?
he loves me.
He loves me.
I love him?
I love him not?
I love him
I love Him.
A collision of destinies?
Our love ain't enough?

I didn't want to let go.
You said you weren't going anywhere,
yet, walking away.
I want to follow you
into loving arms,
past my fears of what lies ahead.
But you pressed hard
against my heart.
"We're not in the same place", you said.
But I take you with me always.

SOPHIA RENEE

        into my dreams.
      You are in my world.
I want to give you the key to my universe.

Myspace and White Chocolate

This was my attempt to find my place in the space of another. Pushing through the ignominious fringe, finding what I dare say could be called a diamond opportunity in this tough, cold turf we call Earth. A precious jewel strong enough to shed the slough of the heart, pairing my slice of life with his, long enough to be rewarded with the endearing phrase, "You are my friend. You are my lover."

Social networking: die-hard shackles suspended in the air by the fantasy and flight of the chat window. Fusing our realities, forgetting for the moment about the maladies in our very different worlds on the other side of the windowpane. Traveling with my mind's eye down the road of possibilities, could he see beyond the pigmented me that he caressed so feverishly as he pressed his tongue deep inside to savor the flavor of my....tonsils? Could he see the heart of me that has no color? The part of me that becomes us with every thrust. No, this was not the norm. But for a moment, normal to us like rain in a quiet storm. Until our high was worn (out) like a faded baseball cap and bid us farewell in the mourn. Gone are our budded lenses that nulled our pointers and lulled our senses. Gone is our liquid courage that pushed our index out of bounds. Pushing enough to shed the slough of your heart and you dared to share a slice of your life with me, long enough to reward me with the endearing phrases, "You are now my awkward friend. You are my lover-perpetually-pending-confirmation". Prevailing was my emotional constipation caused by dehydration from consternation that we had crossed the line.

Now hung-over, strewn thick with thoughts of regret. You soon fret that you did not get what you bet—on. But who was the person that you met? A desirable, lovable, huggable, suckable, fuckable, strong, confident, intelligent, funny, compassionate, humble, exciting, electric, poetic, faithful, loyal, sensual, flexible, approachable, spiritual, and resourceful woman. Parts moving, yet under construction. At times, vulnerable to emotional abduction. Indeed, I was captured and swooned as we jammed to the Chuck Brown tunes. The feelings were surreal, and I made no room for thoughts of no trespassing signs ... until you planted one between us.

I didn't know what to feel, what to do.
Dude, I have feelings just like you.
Who you think the sun gon' shine for, boo?
Don't crush the seed about to bloom in you.
You could be free and loving it too.
But you wanna act like you in a zoo.
All caged up inside and blue.
Here's a little secret: I still got love for you, too.
Cause ain't no harm done, true.
A momentary setback is all I knew.

We gon' be just fine, me and you.
Next time you'll know what to do.

My eyes are wide open now and I don't like what I see. Time to change the scenery. Positivity must become my proclivity. Start by only making time for the worthy. The one who's truly changing....is me.

Lesson learned: question everything. I don't care how paranoid people may describe you. your time, energy, and space in life are worth an interrogation or two for people who want to exist in it.

SOPHIA RENEE

Limits (For Baseball Man)

Do you know
how I feel?

Would this world
understand?

Present laws
do not allow.

Our theorem
has not been
proven.

But the quadrants
of my heart say,

If not in this dimension,
then, to infinity,

in my dreams.

Home

I awakened from my sleep,
troubled at the thought of
a life not walking beside you.

Weaving soul and spirit in time.
Like a mother's scent will not
evade the senses of her child.
The love inside will not run
into a corner and cover its eyes.

Our truth is not blinding,
yet it is unknown to this space.

So, I pray that God's grace
will gently stretch our souls
and guide us as we surrender,

to the home we long to have
in each other's hearts
forever.

SOPHIA RENEE

The Cycle of Letting Go

miss u ... love u ... want u ... need u
u live ... u hurt ... u learn ... u grow

see me ... feel me ... know me ... forgive me ...
2 sides ... 2 lessons ... 2 much ... 2 let go

find your way ...learn to stay ...but not give away ...
who you are ...

trust what God ... called in you ... bury the seed ...
and wait for spring ...

to love again

Katrina

I go to sleep thinking about you.
Wake up thinking about you.
You are the air I breathe and the taste on my tongue.

No time for putting up fences.
You have penetrated my senses and torn down my walls.

My waves of pain pour through and cause me to shake like troubled waters rising when the Nola levees break.

And I sit on top of the house watching the casualties of my past float by.

Waiting for a sign that says,

"This is the last day you cry."

SOPHIA RENEE

Soul Ties

I made love to you today
on your side of the bed.

Did you feel me?

I saw your face.
I felt your energy.
I drowned in the sound
of our auras wrapped and crowned
in passion.

Did you hear me?

I shed tears mourning us.
I look back through time to find
what were the ties that seemed to bind
me down
and keep us connected,
like lovebugs crashing into chrome grills.

Did you see me?

I looked in your eyes,
frozen in a gaze,
paralyzed as time sat in a corner

and watched me coil into hibernation
and weave a cocoon of reflection.

Did you miss me?

Some parts I miss
and some I gladly release.
Yet I must believe that
the process is not about
how one continues to reject
and retreat from me.
It is about how I continue
to do this to myself.

Grateful for the lesson,
for the passion,
for the stretching,
for the journey.

Did I know me?

Not fully.

But I will.

SOPHIA RENEE

ALPJTJ

We clicked Day 1.
And I took a deep breath.
As the air of romance filled my lungs.

Reaching out, I took a nibble
of the fruit of his lips.
I had forgotten how sweet
'Nothings' were.

My womanhood awakened.
Stimulating my mind.
Captivating my soul.
Pulse racing.
Driving me crazy.
I'm so afraid. No, terrified.
But can't wait for his call.

Excited about.
Intrigued.
Inviting the possibilities
With my new best friend.

I, Since You

I want to cry.
The thought of a love so intense frightens me.
Afraid to fall.
Don't let me hit the ground.
Bruised again.

But, since you:
my heart swells at the very thought of you,
my eyes sense the beauty in your smile,
my ears hear the melody of your voice,
my nostrils inhale our fragrant passion erupting from within.

A touch, and then, a taste of passion.
A sensual foretaste of transcending erotica.
Two souls dancing.
Our fabrics interwoven.
Making art together.
I sense you.

This is I, since you.

SOPHIA RENEE

Love Is a Flower

If, by some miracle, I were allowed to pick you,
I would feel like a murderer of souls
and the greediest of bastards
for quenching my thirst,
with one who came to
coat the tongues of
all who share his
space with his
intoxicating
elixir of
love.

God, grant me gracious access to my yet unseen power.
To taste but don't touch; see but don't take,
inhale, savor, and exhale and not go back to look for
or excessively and obsessively mourn that breath.
It is not gone forever, but is recycled and renewed,
if I allow it to be reborn from the walls of my surrender.

This is the new story I choose to write.
choosing a suffer/*sucka*-free life.
Because the alternative sucks.
I cradle myself. Discovering
and getting to know the
fullness and richness

of my love.
She is there. And
she burns all
my edges and
insides raw.
She prevails.
She remains.
And renders
me forever
free.

SOPHIA RENEE

JOURNEY TO SOPHIA, PART II
Spirituality, Sexuality & Erotica

It feels like nothing is left. Nothing that I recognized as myself or having any semblance of the life that I once thought I knew. I say 'thought' because the past couple of months have caused me to question everything I identified as a part of my existence. At first, it felt like I was lying in a pool of my own blood, waiting for my last breath. How crass of me to think that I would know what imminent death feels like, in the physical, that is. Yet, my spirit, my will, my heart, and my mind all feel like I have entered the realm of a place that is so dark, that the other side must be the brightest and boldest of light; new life bursting forth out of darkness. But, instead of relinquishing my grip and surrendering to the demise of the parts I call *me*, each day I pilgrimage to the scene of the crime. I climb back into the chalk-drawn outline of my corpse and listen to the soundtrack filled with melodies of maladies, hoping to discover and re-mix it to fix the wrong note. But I can't get back that track. Notes falling and hanging from their staff with no desire to stay on key. The bottom note fell a long time ago and said, "it's time to rest." I got poetic for a minute, but...shit, I feel like I've been dropped off in a foreign country and each step, each thought, each breath is borrowed. Time has become both irrelevant and immediate. There is so much inside me that wants to get outside and roll around in the grass, or fly, or sit still and breathe fully. A part of me wants to keep playing this broken record—this familiar and painful score. And the volume control is stuck at 100. I feel very alone, lost, paranoid and confused, like my next breath might be my last breath. But, each time I inhale, new air enters my lungs and I want to reserve the moment, because it is the most comfortable space I can find nowadays. Yet, in this space, the perception of safety is often superseded by a treacherously looming defeat. India Arie encourages us to do it, but how do I *break the shell*?

So much of our lives are driven by the success or failure of our love relationships. Why does our involvement with another human being consume so much of our focus, energy, power and our resources?

We ache for it. We search for it. We fight for it. We die for it. L-O-V-E. Without it, we feel a lack of purpose and a lack of significance. We feel empty. A life without connection is not living. The trouble with the perception of some is the layers upon layers of bullshit that we allow to shroud pure love like the smog over California.

I feel myself withdrawing again, knowing fully that this is not the answer. This only feeds the cycle of denial and pain. I am cold and distant toward family members, especially my mother. Of course, the only time I recall us having a close relationship was when I was a little girl. Back then, I remember her always going somewhere and me wanting her to stay. My heart feels like it freezes over with ice when I hear her voice. I hugged my sister on New Year's after watching the ball drop. I felt nothing.

On the heels of a breakup, still looking for work, a myriad of emotions fills my mind. Feeling like I'm in the crossfire of my own words, experiences, discoveries, realizations, and *aha* moments. I feel conflicted and filled to the brim. A good salt bath with some candles and incense, as the prelude to a good cry, would be heavenly now.

But I have things to do! Ain't nobody got time for tears.

Right?

Funny how my goal has mostly been to survive the struggle, to stay "functional" for someone's sake (kids, family, significant other). I am now asking myself if I'm heading towards a victim mentality.

looks for the nearest detour

This section of the collection recalls an intersection to that part of the process where I am sorting out my feelings, intentions, and purpose again. I am either at the beginning of another downward spiraled life lesson or on the cusp of a breakthrough. The bath will have to wait until after the kids are in bed. Suck it up, woman!

I had not realized until this past year how much of my actions, thoughts, and beliefs are driven or induced by fear. Right now, I am terrified at the thought of being alone again. I am feeling like a failure. Feeling like I've been down this road before. I set on a path a year ago to "find myself" and to "free myself" from all the boxes I perceive that I allowed others to put me in, wondering what happened and where I lost my way. I want to go away. I'm not sure where, but away from here.

Have you ever wondered what your life would look like if you just didn't give a fuck? Understanding that I am not in control of anyone but myself, and, hopefully, I am not detached from reality in a way that renders me incapable of controlling myself within reason, why am I so attached to how situations unfold or how people behave in my life? I hear the phrases, *love without condition, unconditional love, do not be attached to the outcome*, and immediately try to reconcile those concepts with the fact that we are born in need of love, attention, and affection, appreciation, and validation. We are born this way!

Where do we draw the line between our need for love and *being* love? Is there a line or is this a measure of the maturity of our existence relative to our awareness of what love is? Tina Turner wrote the song, "What's Love Got to Do With It?" One could argue that she was very angry, hurt, and broken when she wrote this song, thus, her perspective of love was certainly skewed. Another writer spoke from a different view: "The greatest thing you'll ever know is just to love and be loved in return."

Fear. Need for control. Serenity prayer. Release. Peace. Love.

Last night, I was in a state of confusion, flux, anxiety, and uncertainty, seeking answers and direction. Previously, I was focusing on spiritual flow purely from a Christian perspective and I was flooding my psyche with music, tweets from motivational sources, and the 'Sonya-version' of prayers, thoughts, and intentions throughout the day. I felt like I needed movement, but I wasn't clear about which direction I was headed. I was hungry. I'd been hungry for days since the breakup. It seemed that, since he is no longer charting my course, I am searching for something to help move me toward my true path. I can sense that the years of feeling inadequate and fearful are quickly crumbling. I am trying to trace in my mind when I think the breakthrough began, to identify the pattern that existed to support such growth and fortitude. The space that I am in right now is a long time coming. It is the culmination of many tears that have fallen from my eyes, many conversations and moments of deep, reflective thought, many positive messages inside and outside the church, and a deep longing to stop merely surviving. No more functioning in low gear. I am ready to stop surviving and begin to embrace and experience life fully. Self-acceptance has colored my thoughts lately. I am beginning to regard myself with more kindness. I feel less of me trying to sell, convince, explain, submit myself for approval, and obtain validation from other people.

SOPHIA RENEE

Go Within

We would rather not see others' ugly parts.
We don't even like seeing our own.
The colors of life don't always stay in the lines.
Maybe it's time to get a new box of crayons.
Fully bleed 'till you are empty.
Make room for shapes and colors
that can only be seen with new eyes.
Hands glued to the knob of continuous
doors you have walked through before.
Lot's wife looked back—salt she became.
Dust and ashes of old flames and spaces.
pave the way to blissful graces.
You must first face your demons.
Only you can light your way.
A beautiful death and resurrection.
Go within to create the connection
to the Source, the All.
The promise of perfection
lies between the cracks of your heart.
Trust enough to clear the rough
and dirty stuff that no one sees
but you and God.
You are a masterpiece.
Underneath a sheath of pretentious pomp.
Lay it to rest.
For it is best
to live a clean life
than to die inside a delicious corpse.

Cocoon

I wish I didn't like to taste her so much.
'cause I need a father for my children.
lost.

The snowman never vacations.
wrong number?
for now.

When I open my eyes,
I think of you.
I want to dive into your love.

I held you in my space beyond your season.
dis-ease.

Shivering naked in the winter of my soul.
My soul cried for you.
Empty.

I remember the wallpaper in this place.
Peeled and torn edges.

Thinking about thinking.

Feeling the shift outside of myself.

SOPHIA RENEE

Separation.
Isolation.
Desolation.

Reaching for His hand.
Letting go.
Releasing to embrace.

Leaves about to turn.
Fall is near.
Shedding into life.
Ready for the rebirth.

Forward motion.
Searching for my own groove.
Ever-changing and evolving.
Regroup.

Fear is my shadow.
Fingertips stretching for the Light.
Switch.

Praying for the turn.
Listening for the voice.
Careful steps.
I press.

Turning inward.
Repelling outward.
I build the wall.
I must believe in the process.

To Be Continued ...

SOPHIA RENEE

Lost

I want to drown
in the sound
of silence and caterpillars.

No map.
GPS is on the brink of blinking.
Attitude is stinking.

Thinking that I'm reaping
seeds sown while I was creeping.

Creeping in the night
for what can only be found in the Light.

I don't like the life I'm living,
but it's the only one I've got.

Every time I turn around,
I turn around and I ask myself
"Why am I just surviving'?"

Then I remember:
I was the one driving!

Driving my life away to get away,

find a way to lay
to getaway,
to get a way.

Wanting my high to stay just another day.

No money to pay
the piper
to put down his pipe.

Suffocating,
Thinking my next frame is deflating.

Wondering why we lie
to satisfy
the nothingness gone awry.

Why does my shit have to rhyme?
My wit just doesn't fit.

My expressions seem to elude
the flow of melodic rivers

from the orifices of my black brothas and sistas.

I get stuck in time
trying to rewind
only to find that

SOPHIA RENEE

I've passed that tree
three times three
times already.

Jaded at the hope un-gripped
of my lips being worthy to press

against the cup of life
and drink,
piercing through my strife

and bringing my staccato
to rest.

Grow In Grace

Living out our fantasies
instead of creating our realities.
Clinging to our suffering
instead of living a life of ease.

Chasing a heart's caress
instead of loving ourselves the best.
Taking only what is given *(crumbs)*
instead of getting to the living.

Big girls don't run, they rise.
Soaring up to see the prize (Philippians 3:14).
Realizing the very thing you chase,
abides in the secret place
of the Most High.

And the breath you take
is the path you create.
Diving into the stillness
of pure consciousness.
The abyss of nothingness
and more than enough.

To rest and just
Be.

SOPHIA RENEE

Letter to Little Sophia

I know you are scared to look *inside.*
You're still looking for something.
Waiting to be seen,
heard,
vindicated and validated.
Wanting to be somebody's world,
but carrying your pain
like souvenirs hanging from keychains
or that folded money grandma used to pull from her bosom.
They weren't supposed to touch you there
and leave you alone
without a care.
I see you stealing moments of bliss.
Those days when you dare not miss
the opportunity to feel God's kiss.
Catching a glimpse of your perfection,
longing to loosen your grip
on the scales of justice
and peel back
the crust from your eyes,
revealing the disguise
of a lie that's taken hold for too long.
I'm writing you this letter
because I want to give you that extra hug.
Show you how it feels for me to tug

on your skirt
and teach you the ways of womanhood
and how he should honor you.
let you know that the best of you
is seeking you,
is waiting to know you,
is waiting to show you
how to put your fears to rest.
Come.
Lay your head on my chest.
Feel my arms surround you,
squeeze you and tell you
I won't run away.
Tarry with me
another hour to pray
till the scars fall away
and there's nothing left
but love.

SOPHIA RENEE

You Won't Lose

In my alone time,
I feel god's presence expanding within me
like gentle gusts of air flowing into my heart/lungs.
Right at the moment when I feel that I cannot receive another drop,
I am stretched and filled over and over again.
Feeling taller,
lighter,
higher.
I can breathe if I feel like it ... or not.
My cup is overflowing.
I am a river of joy.
Surrender.
You won't lose.
Asé. Amen. Aho.

Spiritual Midwives

They labored with us,
holding us in the light of love
as we purged our darkness and pain.

They held our hands
and cradled our hearts
while spirit washed
our ugly parts
with consuming fire
from the Goddess of Love
and healing waters
soft as a dove.

They labored with us,
pouring into our spirit
as we purged our darkness and pain.

They covered us
and carried us through
while our streaming tears
flowed into our truth
that bliss is waiting,
waiting on us,
with joy unspeakable
longing to heal us

SOPHIA RENEE

and fill our cups
after purging our pain
with boundless love
breaking our chains.

They labored with us,
and together we opened our hearts
as we purged our darkness and pain.

They labored with us,
endured with us,
loved on us,
protected us,
and we died
to live again.

Waking Up

Sometimes waking up feels like breaking up.
Splitting hairs between up and down.
Giving my soul the run around.
Looking for breadcrumbs on the ground.
These clues ain't blue.
They're looking for you.
What's your hurry, child?
Sit. Down.

Doing The Work

Journey into myself.
The darkness and the light.
Shadows dancing beyond plain sight.
Ancient sounds and rhythms in flight.
Breath resting in the sacred corners of night.
Guide my return home.
This knowing is my birthright.
Selah.

Bars From the Matrix

light and darkness
swinging in the tree
seems like y'all stay
fucking with me
need to get still
blue or red pill
open my heart
so my eyes can see

Growth (Haiku)

Shifting toward greatness.
My world converging with source.
I am the journey.

Present

There once was a girl named Patience.
The more she waited, the more it felt like a meditation,
a dance,
story time,
a great lesson.
She gave herself permission to be okay in her now moments.
For, they all conspired to bring her to places far beyond where
her anxious mind could ever take her.

You Got This

When the tears come,
let them wash away all that your soul
has grown weary of carrying.
Let them renew your spirit
for the journey ahead.
You will not drown
or become overtaken by them.
Trust that God is watching
while your soul is washing.
Rest in his love.
You got this.

SOPHIA RENEE

Fall

When you feel like the walls
are pushing back at you,

reach up and let the wind
lift you.

When your feet seem bolted to the floor,
stretch your arms like branches

and listen to the birds
sing you a love song.

When your leaves bark about leaving,
cast your eyes on their colors

as they dance to the prelude
of your new world.

Heart Poetry

Swimming in a spiritual sea.
Surrounded by a myriad of creatures.
Dark, murky waters in certain spaces.
Longing to rise to the surface and the light.
Yet, to a certain depth, I am drawn.
Winding through the shadow-filled corridors
of my mind.
The monsters in my head sing a chorus
but the light holds my heart
and pulls me closer
beyond my fear.
Knowing what I have determined to do
I prepare to enter the soft and most secret place
I remember in the womb.
I tap the mic and say, "Is this thing on?"
Finding my voice
as I hear from source,
I speak truth to my heart—

Let go.
Believe in yourself.
Be free.
and remember,

You are Love.

SOPHIA RENEE

Manifesto

I am living well
on purpose.

I am living,
laughing, and loving
out loud.

I embrace my own, ever-evolving truth and
follow it passionately,
pressing through my fears.

Conquering them, one by one,
waving as I pass them by.
Leaving a trail of tears sprinkled
with jewels of laughter.

Not dictating the outcome,
I trust the process.

Stirring

My insides are perpetually stirring.
Things feel like they are reconciling inside of me energetically.
For once I am willing to see everything as it is and
allow things to happen to process, heal and move forward.

This is divine intelligence,
beyond what my mind can comprehend.
I've witnessed it happening and I can't explain its logic.
Everything points to action.

"Take all this goodness and what is happening to you, and
apply it to your life, and then to the lives of those around you,
even the ones who seemed difficult to show love and
compassion to before."

Awakening (Ode to John)

Just before dawn,
the moon stirs your waters
and draws you into my ocean.

Your hands exploring my hills and valleys.
My lady parts soaking up your love.
Awakening my forgotten,
yet slumbering senses.

Music flowing through my cells,
cooing me with
the song of the lover.

Watering my lotus flower.
Creating a swelling sensation
mounting from the inside.

Your caress softens my petals
and I sway in the gentle wind
that is you.

Naked

He held me
and I cried
and cried.

He opened my heart
so big and wide.

All I could do
was be.

SOPHIA RENEE

A Drop of Water

Held me through the uncertainties and dark, fearful spaces
Tears erupting from deep within,
carrying with them years of the dregs
from the agony of self-denial.
Almost like torture, to constantly peek at the promised land
and say, "that's not for you. not yet."
My chest feels congested, arrested. frozen.
from holding back. but what was I holding it for?
It gets so heavy.
Suddenly... Like I forgot I was carrying it.
A big ol' *sike!*
Laughing in my face as beads of sweat
from my toiling grow larger.
I thought I was on a journey. Now I'm lost again.
Somebody ate my crumbs.
Then I remember I got hungry along the way.
I was in a hurry to find peace of mind.
"Like a drop of water wondering about
its place in the ocean", he said.
And, in that tearful moment, I exhaled, and I let go.
And then, I rested.
I love you.

Archaeology

Sweeter.
Deeper.
Higher.
Fire.
You have journeyed the landscape of my soul.
Touched my ruined parts and breathed new life and love into me.

Unearthed, rebirthed, and preserved my delicate flower.
You renew within me a thirst for my greater and bring peace to my mind.
That's what you do to me by just being.

Your very existence is spiritual medicine in every way.
The more I can see my greatness in your reflection,
The more air fills my lungs with possibilities and power.

Hello, Sir. Render

My sweet Sir. Render awaits.
that moment when I unleash
the sensual, soulful cries of passion.
Pressing against the edge of my soul.

Your spirit beckons through time and space.
No barrier can hold you from my heart.
No medium too complex to carry
your message of desire.

Love awaits my embrace.
That little girl/grown woman
at the same time kind of love.

Pure, almost timid, in your presence.
A wanting and knowing
of what lies on the other side
of my pride, my fear, my pain.

The dream leaves a sweet taste
on my tongue.
Intoxicated.
Suspending my senses
to awaken at the appointed time.
Spirit-induced coma.

When your mouth speaks,
my body trembles.

I become like a child
wanting to be held,
knowing your arms are waiting
to cover me, caress, and care for me.

Usher me into my higher existence.
Draw me across the troubled waters of fear,
to my place of peace, pleasure, and power.
Enticing me beyond my self-doubt
to the sublime serenity of unconditional love.

Your bedside manner
pulsates from my root to my crown.
I am floating inside myself
giddy in anticipation of
the next frame of persuasion.

Your love swells within me,
pressing against my tired, worn, tattered skin
as it expands through my being.
I am healed, I am restored, I am made whole.

Hello, Sir. Render.
I am delighted to be yours

528 Hertz

Your love shakes up everything inside me.
It dispels those things that block, mute, or mask the true me
and beckons my I Am to breathe again.
I know it is love moving through you and me.
The love frequency has no container, only conduits.

Kintsukuroi

Inside out. I am undone.
A mess pile of humanity.
Shining through the cracks of my heart.
Feeling the warmth and safety of your love.
A beautiful butterfly emerging.
Fresh like morning dew.
The aroma of fresh flowers drapes my nostrils as I spread my wings and fly.

Titillation

My Kundalini
comes out to play
in the sandbox made
from wet pools of
rippling soft currents
and fairy flights
in waves
of you.

Marinate

I will marinate while I wait
to press my lips softly against yours.

I will marinate while I wait
to lay my head upon your chest,
swirl my love energy into yours.

I will marinate while I wait
for you to dive into my ocean,
swim in my waters,
and drink from my cavern of bliss.

I will marinate while I wait,
for the beat of your drum
to summon the rhythm in my hips and thighs.
call me to my highest frequency.

I will marinate while I wait,
chanting the tones that our hearts sing together
to find our way home in each other's hearts,
in trance.

I will marinate while I wait
and be ready for you to wrap yourself
around me like a warm blanket
on a rainy night with the windows open,
laying in front of the fire.

while I wait, I will marinate.

Hearts Open

We swirled heart energy between our souls
like rain washes the forest.

and I laid down the fight in me
like a worn rag doll that I had outgrown.

his hands cradled my body while his lips
pollinated my soul with fresh possibilities.

I returned to myself like an old friend as we bathed in a
microcosmic orbit of unbridled yet, purposeful intention.

our blended aroma smelled of love, glazed with a touch of lust,
as we raised the stakes right through our hearts.

Torque

Playful interaction.
Deep shares on life.
Laughter like medicine.
Ida and Pingala twirling figure eights.
Perpetually piqued by this gravitational pull.

The Awakening of Sophia

He held on to me
while I let go.
He patiently and lovingly filled my edges with warmth,
anchoring my soul
into the depths of my surrender.
Washing me with my own tears.
He remained,
as I shed my callused skin.

Defeated demons purging
My softer emerging.
He covered and carried me
to the space beyond my yearning.
Inscribing ancient lessons into
my open heart.
Satisfying my lips
with the sweetness of becoming.

My lotus flower blooming
bursting forth with a knowing
of the answer to my calling.
Marinating in the river of oneness,
I am awakened,
to remember.

Shavasana

My core is the door to sacred spaces.
Your touch leaving sweet traces
of truth in sound.

Feels familiar these places
and the hint of what the heart encases,

leading us to a place where
lifting each other up,
is the only way we get down.

Behind the bushes like shadows creeping
till your presence makes what was lost—
found.

No secrets worth keeping,
pages of my heart opened like a book.
Reclaimed my time and everything they took.

With the light, you chant down Babylon in my soul.
Ida and Pingala spinning 8s in gold.
Jeremiah said it's like fire.
Your appetite is my desire.

Out from the mud,
behold my lotus flower spread,

to crown your godhead,
with grace for a long and tedious race.

Raining down visions of ending staccato
Breathing aligning,
until our masks give birth to faces.

No more remaining to be held.
Final resting pose.

Exhale.

SOPHIA RENEE

Grapes and Shit

From the moment my feet shared the space
where he laid his head,
I felt his intentions deep inside me.

Even as I tried to resist
and cover the cold, exposed,
and most vulnerable parts of myself,
he gently and deliberately undressed me.

Despite my attempts to invoke the usual detours,
he lovingly persisted.
Calling, conjuring, and drawing me closer
with sounds of freedom and original frequencies
my ears had forgotten
or resigned from hearing.

Something within me yearns for this
thirsts for this.
My insides ache.
I feel parched and barren.

His voice echoed through my spirit
like a bass drum reminding my soul
of the rhythm of my heartbeat.

LOVE NOTES FROM, SOPHIA

Tones reverberating and resonating
until the dam breaks
and my walls cannot contain
the rivers of my sorrow.

As he speaks his message
to the depths of my valleys
and bids to me straighten up
to dive over what feels like
the edge of myself,
a steep cliff
over which
I would surely die.

This is how I perceive the other side of my comfortable existence
the, *don't rock the boat, 'cause I got shit to do* cliff

I portray that I am confused
on what my most authentic self looks and feels like.
Or is that an illusion I have created?

In the same vein, I am so touched and intrigued
by how sweet and powerfully his love shows up
to meet my fears, patterns, and programs,
with a reverent demand
that only speaks to my higher self.

SOPHIA RENEE

Peeling away my collection of masks
of frailty and spiritual resign.
Redirecting my interference with a persistent truth
that knows I can be better.
He has seen it.
And he knows I have, too.

I want to swim in his waters forever.
But that would not be where my story becomes *my story*.
I hear his words echoing in my mind.
No more fading conveniently into the backgrounds of life's frames.
Time to bring my whole ass to the stage.

I'd rather sleep than show up.
I want to extend my hand to the corner
and tag my imaginary partner into the ring.
Because I often feel like I can't handle the demands of living.

Truth is, I am afraid to witness those who cannot (or do not) appreciate my flavor.
My specific brand of doing life.
Consequently, I have devalued and muted myself in certain circles because I have ranked my worth among the group and decided I didn't belong
or was not worthy of being in the room.
The lies we tell ourselves.

But he loved on me.
He sliced my grapes, laid them across a bed of spinach and tomatoes and glazed them with a sweet, tangy balsamic vinaigrette.
Surely, this was an orgasm in a bowl!

He also told me I was "full of shit"…and, at least I know it.
Spiritual credit? nah!
He saw straight inside of me and I really like him being there.
He won't let me rest until I get to the best part of me.
Moving beyond awareness alone and into the fullness, flavor, and color that I uniquely bring
to each stroke of my pen, brush against my canvas,
stirring of my pot on the stove,
the plucking of my guitar strings, thrusting of my hips,
tone of my voice,
and whatever other things fill my lungs with air and bring me joy.

Now what am I going to do?

Acquire my own taste
and dare to be.

SOPHIA RENEE

Lotus Flower

My lotus flower is blooming.
Soft, yet, fiery petals of pleasure
moistened with anticipation of that moment
when your tongue glides gently across my lips
and your nostrils are filled with my aroma.

My lotus flower is blooming.
The mere presence of your manhood
awakens my great-er-ness.
I become filled with the call of my ancestors
beckoning me to rise in ecstasy and fulfill my purpose.

My lotus flower is blooming
Visions of fleshly, animalistic passion
unleashes my otherwise guarded nature,
causing my insides to tremble and moan
with an unspeakable depth of desire.

My lotus flower is blooming.
I ache for you to penetrate and eliminate the layers.
Layers that we have worn become torn.
They fade and give way to our godly form.

My lotus flower is blooming.
Do you thirst for this elixir?

Are you open for the journey to the heart fixer?
Come travel with me through the seven dimensions of love.

Let's dive into each other
and meet our eternal selves.
Commune as gods until we have
manifested a masterpiece of magnificence
as one.

SOPHIA RENEE

More Please

Let's do it again.
Wrap ourselves up in each other's intentions and love.
Lose our inhibitions and fears to divine will and providence.

Invite God to the center of the sweet spot created
between our hearts,
into the depths of our souls,
choreographed and cradled in tents under the full moon.

Giving rest to our burdens carried across the rivers of our tears.
Shed our fears.
There is no wrong way to sing our song.

With bellowing, hope-filled lungs and sweet whispers
of mercy and truth.
Melting away our shadows just before the dawn.
And God smiles as our prayers say Amen.

Those Hands

I am still thinking of those arms and hands stretched wide on top of mine, and that deep, soft whisper to "go there" because I deserved it. I need those hands. I ache for those hands. My insides are still trembling.

I confess that my satisfaction is truly fueled by these *proxy* experiences. I know who I really want to carry out these assignments, but all I need to do is close my eyes, imagine, and I am filled to overflowing with delicious ecstasy.

I love his smile and those knowing eyes. I never thought that orgasm could be achieved without totally focusing on physical stimulation. Of course, the *surrogate* was a key player. But I was enraptured by our moans, the caressing, and the way our grips spoke to each other.

I purposefully kept my eyes closed and imagined the object of my true desire. I imagined who I really wanted to part my thighs and bury his head between my gates of passion. The surrogate's tongue seemed to quiver across my puss in a darting motion. And with each stroke, my back arched upward to fully position myself to experience this treat.

I licked my lips with anticipation that I would soon be able to wrap them around my mentor's loins.

SOPHIA RENEE

QOTD

Juicy dew-dripped-pussy-petals
are the perfect bed for you to lay your face.
Pay homage with every coin to her fountain.
She'll rain on your universe and move mountains
like they never existed.

Catch all my rain
Don't drown in my pain.
Hold me through it
While I anchor to my joy.

Sweet kisses true.
Casting shadows in the light.
Dancing for this tasty delight.

And the souls of our flesh.
enjoined and screaming *yes*.

I surrender to your care.
take me there.

I am aching and marinating
and waiting...

Heart Sex

Her heart and pussy are smiling.
When the heart and pussy are resonating together,
it creates a vortex of love and deeply intense pleasure.
A reverberating resonance with Source.

It is possible to immerse yourself
and deeply penetrate another's spirit and soul
and anchor yourself inside of her.

Her heart remembers the joy of this space and commands her pussy
to expand her gateways to pleasure.
She opens her spirit deep and wide to let you in.

You aim your thrust straight through her heart, to the point that
she feels like she's being
fucked from the inside out.

She melts into the love puddle you have conjured from her
and prays more prayers that this prayer
would never end.

Because right now is right.
And right is what she is craving right now.
For a thousand eternities, now is all she has.

And she's choosing now
with you.

SOPHIA RENEE

Oral Surgery

He licked each lip,
and gently sucked the head.

I arched my pelvis forward to meet his tongue—
confirming he is in the right place.
I held on to his head and massaged his ears, guiding his thrust
to my palace of pleasure.

This also created a circle of connection/energy between us.
I imagined a white light flowing slowly
from his mouth to my yoni.
I chanted "send me the light" over and over.

My pleasure mounted toward its peak.
I chanted, "my pussy is filled with gratitude" again and again.
My cavern of bliss exploded with love juices
and his moans modulated with mine as he drank to his delight.

He persists until I am fully his,
until my face is covered with tears of surrender.

Bedtime

My insides, ache.
My nipples, ripe.
Fruit ready to burst
and drizzle her juices
around your tip.

Feel my lips
glide in motion
with my hips
and cradle your lingam.
Goodnight.

Stroking your canvas with colors
dripping from my b(r)ush.
basting neural pathways with wet, white light
shining against soft petals.

Blooming and oozing and *dew*-ing.
Sending waves of I Am until you say Amen.

# Welcome Home

He's a good kisser. And I love the way his hands felt all over my body. He started caressing me as soon as he walked through the door. I dressed up for him in a red and yellow-flowered, crinkled tube top with a matching sarong. I wore panties because the little red corvette was still parked in my driveway. I had given him a heads up about our little *constraint* and he said that we still had other options. I was excited to experience my options with him.

We went upstairs and, as I took each step, he kissed me on the neck and caressed me from behind. he always asks me "What do you want me to do, baby?" The pleaser in me has no clue about asking for specifics up front, but I do recognize when I like something. I tell him to just be creative and that he will have to orchestrate this symphony. He says he wants to fuck my mouth. I absolutely love to kiss and suck on a good dick. I lay on the bed with my head hanging just over the edge and he glides into my mouth shortly after I greet his cock with a kiss.

I kiss and lick around the head, then I take it all in and tickle the back of my throat to show him that I will let it go all the way. I slide it out as I give him my famous swirl-suck, basically swirling my tongue around his tool from the base to the head and topping it off with a long, hard suck. His moans become more audible and he's calling me his baby now. He is ready to fuck my mouth now and he leans over and takes charge with a gentle thrust at first. Then his thrusts became more rhythmic and determined. I could feel his swollen dick taking up all the space in my mouth. I stretched it wide to take all that he wanted to give. I gently massaged his sac and began to play with my nipples. I let out a gagged moan and he discovered that I was getting excited as well.

I secretly wanted him inside of me. He must have sensed my longing because he asked me if were okay. I laid down a towel and he slowly slid on top of me, landing near my breasts. My nipples were as hard as bullets by now. He barely touched them with the palm of his hands, and I arched toward him with delight. He liked the way that my nipples were so sensitive. He began kissing and sucking on my breasts and I felt his warm body press against mine. I closed my eyes and imagined what it would be like to have this kind of pleasure all the time.

He kissed me between my breasts and then down the middle one kiss after another until he reached my panties. "Take them off", he said in a soft whisper. His voice set my insides afire. I peeled off my panties and threw them over the bed. "Be gentle", I said. (I was still in a delicate condition.) He lowered into me with compassion. We embraced in the moment, as if our bodies were saying to each other "Welcome Home".

SOPHIA RENEE

Longing

Have you ever felt it
deep in your heart?
in your soul?
Have you ever been read
like the greatest story ever told?

Have you ever slid your hands
across her body like braille?
Following the roadmap
through her heaven and hell?

Traversing the curse in her universe.
Dispersing blessings in her sweet thing
to bring her sorrow to an end.
Begin the mending of her broken heart.
proving it was a setup from the start.

You closed your eyes instead of seeing
the lies of separation and gloom.
Her delicious flowers now bloom.

Nectar never tasted like this.
That sticky, yummy dewy you missed.
Gliding your thickness in deep.
Then, seal it with a kiss.

Sticky

Tonight, I am feeling like I want slow, hot, steamy sex.
Feeling the heat from flesh
rubbing against mine.
I want it to get sticky.
So sticky, we both need a shower.
The water caresses and smooths out our desire,
giving way to our hands on each other's bodies,
heating up again quickly,
and I feel a finger slowly swirling inside me.
I raise my leg and perch my pussy to increase my pleasure,
and begin to hump the hand that feeds me.
With continued rhythmic thrusts, my pussy is milked for her
sweet, dewy goodness.
I open my mouth to pant heavily like a big cat.
The more I tap into my animalistic nature, the closer I get to
the height of my pleasure.
Instinctively, I grasp the shower bar to support the full weight
of his thrusts.
Fucking what seems to have grown from one finger to, two,
three, and, then, a rock-hard cock.
Feels like the key unlocking my treasures, and my secrets, at the
same damn time.
I am pleasantly overwhelmed and in awe of a beautiful,
synchronous joy as our orgasms embrace.

SOPHIA RENEE

Mix?

DJ dropped the beat so deep, my insides leaked.
Leaving trails and streaks of slutty peaks.
Hills and valleys. go deep. so deep.
What you sow, you shall also reap.
A faithful promise to keep.

Write your name from the astral plane
in a language that my only pussy can speak.
Will you chop my secrets into tiny pieces?
Or will you mix pleasure and pain,
scratching my sweet thang?

My spirit got that itch for a new venue.
These old wineskins won't do.
Always on track when I'm riding you.
Making us catch a flow.
Screw it, 'til I know what to do.

Yes, to you is like agony and the death of my will to thrive.
Staying alive is my only truth.
Yet your elixir drips on my honey pot
like liquid fire licking a sample in my booth.

Keep knocking, you'll reach that back corner pocket.
Venus grip only knows to lock it

And give you what you came for.
Creamy white waves crashing.
The shore, as we knew it, is no more.

Left naked in our shadows.
Grasping for the light.
Praying to the god of rhythm
that our souls would surrender the fight.

Trust that love would fill in the gaps
and sing a new song.
Ad infinitum. And so on.
It was so long
'til the tables were turned.

The flip side is sweet death.
Remixed and returned.
A lesson to learn.
Again and again.
Until it is earned.

"There go that man."
Giving up my plan.
Listening to the Master's.
Please, take my hand.
Through the echoes.

SOPHIA RENEE

Words seeped through my soul and left a mark,
Concealers can't fix or blend.
Only love can mend this broken heart
down below.

If given the chance to defend her,
Would you give space for grace?
Abandon your insolent disregard
of her sovereign place?

She cannot hear unless you
change the frequency of your tune,
love every one of her walls down,
make her flowers bloom.
While freshly dipped honeydew
drips from your lips,
as you taste the truth of her new moon.

An unexpected guest, like Christmas in June,
Her soul engulfed by the light,
Our new name is
One Love.

LOVE NOTES FROM, SOPHIA

SOPHIA RENEE

Tantric Love: An Erotic Short Story

Upon entering his home, our energy instantly synchronizes as we embrace and engage in deep breathing. In stillness, we continue to breathe while circulating the energy between us. As we sink deeper into each other, we begin to rock gently back and forth, entranced by the vortex of Kundalini we are creating. Kisses from his lips all over my face send tremors that trace the deep space between my heart and my pussy until I become ripe with anticipation to feel his mouth all over my body. Still fully clothed, my legs become weak, and my pussy begins to pulsate and throb, opening her lips like the petals of a flower and moistening my crotch with her holy nectar.

    He places his hands firmly against my cheeks and squeezes my ass to let me know I've been a bad girl, and his righteous rod of correction stands ready to deliberate my recompense. With an equal sense of comfort, sliding his hands inside my panties to feel my warm, soft tush, he cups me so gently that I surrender whatever stress, anxiety, and fight that's left inside me from the burdens of the day, and I bury my head into his chest. Tears stream down my face and I let go as much as I know how. "Let it out. I got you, baby," he whispers to let me know I can put my superwoman cape away while I am in his care. The bass in his voice lets me know that, in his arms I am home.

As I continue to release, Kundalini rises once again. Our breathing deepens and our grown parts become magnetized in a subtle but deeply intense grind on each other until, although we are fully clothed, I can feel him inside me! He continues making deliberate thrusts toward my mound and she becomes swollen, wet, and wanting, opening her gates to swallow his auric dick whole. He pumps again and again and sends me slithering like a snake tightening her grip on his body. I feel his righteous rod of correction extend from my pussy up through my heart, and I am moaning and dripping between my legs until I feel a surge coming out of the top of my head. As if one person, we exhale in ecstasy.

He kisses me again on my lips and my forehead, steps back and takes a good look at my freshly orgasmed face, smiles, and gives me time to gather my senses. I leave my shoes at the front door, and he grabs my purse and overnight bag to take upstairs. Intoxicated by the rise in sexual energy, I grip the stair post to ensure I make it to his bedroom door, while he enjoys the view from behind. He places my bags on the lounge chair and asks the question which always gets a yes, "Would you like to go to the window?" We go to the window, and he pulls out a long, glass bong from the cabinet under the sink and places some sativa blend into the reservoir before presenting it to me for the first puff. I place my mouth over the large tip of his big glass bong, and he lights it up while I suck gently to inhale the fragrant bliss vapor into my lungs. I extend the bong to him, flirting with him like we've just met. I will soon be splayed on his platter for devouring in slow, deliberate ways. As we finish our pre-game session and I turn to head back toward his bed, he wraps his arms around me from behind and stops to stare at us in the mirror. He's glad that he has me, even if only for the night. he thinks to himself, "she's all mine."

By now, I am feeling the effects of the Sour OG and I am ready to grant his every wish. Ready to fly on this magic carpet of passion, pleasure, and perhaps, a bit of pain. We embrace yet again and this time he reaches to undo my bra, but notices I am not wearing one. He raises with excitement to know he is that much closer to feeling my soft, supple skin against his swollen hard mansion of manhood. He slowly pulls my blouse over my shoulders, brushing the fabric against my voluptuous breasts and my pants fall to the ground in concert. He slides off his clothes, sits on the side of the bed, and beckons me to lay across his lap. "What time did you say you were going to be here?" I stammer with an innocent grin, "T-ten o'clock." He replies, "Why do you make me wait so long? I'll have to punish you; you know that right?" I nod "Yes," as if to resign in agreement about my disobedience and assume the position.

I lay my fully naked body across his lap, positioning my pussy on top of him so I can at least feel his dick rise as consolation for the spanking my ass is about to endure. He likes to spank me repeatedly to test my boundaries. One-Two-Three. Harder. Four-Five-Six. Rub. Seven-Eight-Nine. Harder. Ten-Eleven-Twelve. Harder. HARDER. I begin to squeal and squirm. He rubs it in to comfort me, then cranks up the rhythm again. I begin to think about the wrong I have done, promise him I'll be a good girl, and it won't happen again. Then, I confess the truth that it might, and he must increase the intensity of my punishment until I can really feel him. I arch my ass up to meet each lick and lock into his rhythm until I melt into the bliss of the blows from his open hand. The sensations are intoxicating, and I begin to squeeze my pussy and cry "Yes, daddy! Spank me some more!" His hands come faster and harder. His delivery of more spanks than rubs sends me into a frenzy, and I moan and squeal as he peppers my punishment with tiny kisses on my ass to let me know it's all love. He raises me up and tells me to lay down on my back and spread my legs.

My mound is already dripping wet from my first two orgasms. He has wanted to taste her since I walked through the door. Of course, a good spanking was both discipline and a reward for the wild child and bad girl in me. He needed to prime and prepare her to receive him willingly. He gently caressed my pussy petals with his tongue from top to bottom, coercing my hips to raise closer for her to meet his mouth. Instinctively, I motioned my pelvis to begin rhythmic flexing to feel his flicking tongue beat my pussy into loving surrender. She is hot, wet, and ready for more.

He rises slowly as if he is full and I asked with a surprised and disappointed look, "Why did you stop?" He tells me, "I know you want some of this big black dick, too." Translation: He is ready for me *now*. He comes closer, hovers over me to enjoy the view and smiles at the beauty spread beneath him. He leans forward to kiss me and brings his hardness close but stops at the door of my cavern of bliss. I open wide to receive and as our lips pressed together in a deep kiss, I begin to feel something penetrate my other lips.

To my surprise, he is still just outside the door! He begins visualizing his manhood penetrating my pussy deeply and repeatedly with slow, rhythmic thrusts of intention and precision. My heater gets hotter and thirsts with anticipation to be filled with more of his god-dick energy, and my hips begin to undulate to receive him. Deeper and deeper. He is somehow energetically inside me and in the same way he feels my lips squeeze as my juices trickle down my thighs.

We begin to gaze in each other's eyes. Our inhales and exhales dance between hearts and our movements come to a steady rhythm of pulse-then-stillness until my floodgates burst open. My boiling honey pot gushes over and soaks the bed.

As if there were anything more that she could take, while I am still orgasming, he slides his dick inside me *for real* and rests in my fire pussy just because. The tremors feel like he is swaddling his dick with my pussy, and he doesn't want to miss witnessing a drop of my pleasure.

He is still hungry and it's time for him to be fed. He lifts me up, lays on his back, and tells me to climb up and sit on his face. My legs are weak like mush at this point, but I have no plans on forfeiting this pussy worship. I straddle his head, spread my lips, and lower myself until I feel his tongue begin to explore my landscape for more orgasms to release.

I rest my pussy on his face, and he munches me delicately like morsels of a gourmet dessert. He is eating me like his life depends on it. He speeds up lapping and licking and I grip the wall and bed rail to anchor myself. He thrusts his tongue inside my pussy and the sensation is so intense. I plant her more firmly on his face until he begins to consider how he might breathe with his ears. He devours me like I'm his first home-cooked meal in years and my moans get louder and louder until my words turn into a growl; more like the purring of a big cat.

I feel as if I have become a feline fantasy getting her pussy sucked and I begin to growl even more as my pussy rages with primal pleasure. Time seems to vanish in the grip of our animalistic indulgence. His licks feel like flesh dipped in liquid fire and my pussy attempts to quench the thirst of this hardworking, dedicated man. With a deep guttural growl, she gushes forth again. This time right into his mouth. He drinks and drinks and gasps and drinks all my elixir. It always makes him stronger. I raise up to dismount and he grabs my leg to plant a final kiss down there as if to say Amen.

I slide beside him, and he grabs me close to him as I melt into his arms. We are content. We are fulfilled. We are one.

SOPHIA RENEE

JOURNEY TO SOPHIA CONTINUES
A Peek into My Chrysalis

Your journey includes the detours.
Honor yourself every step of the way. All is one.
Each day, practice being yourself and loving yourself.
Do it for those who wouldn't or couldn't when you needed it most. It may take a while to get the hang of it,
but you'll get better each time you do.
If you are ready to experience *A Delicious Life*, start by redirecting the energy you have invested into propagating your illusions of "comfort" and using that same power to connect with the real you.
If there is a part of you that continues to choose suffering, find it, face it and love on it until that behavior shifts.
When you are preoccupied with the acceptance of others, consider whether you have fully accepted yourself.
Envision the day when the doctor says,
"Take 200 fire breaths and call me in the morning."

SOPHIA RENEE

About the Author

Sophia Renee is a mother, techie, musician, poet, writer and revolutionary in the areas of self-empowerment, spirituality and sexual freedom. Sophia currently lives in Lawrenceville, Georgia. Her hometown is Tallahassee, Florida where her mother read to her often while she was still in the womb. Her mother's practice of reading to her pregnant belly in the late 60's was certainly a revolutionary act in ushering Sophia's presence into the world as Sonya Renee. Sonya was born on March 21, 1970, through Earnestine and Frank Crimbley with an abundant dose of curiosity-driven spunk. Her parents were divorced when she was at a very young age. While living with her grandparents, she began learning untimely lessons about sex, mental illness and dysfunction from would-be-trusted friends and family, who ripped out the answers from the back of the book, along with her innocence. Sophia managed to find solace in her prayer closet and journals. Her expression via poetic prose began in her adolescent years. The tone was dark and despondent, yet these dark letters helped to pave the road from major depression and suicidal ideation to her present transformation.

Today, Sophia shares her creative energy in whatever form it flows, freely and without fear. She endeavors to empower others in the process. She believes that her purpose is to answer with her life's breath, the question: "Who am I to be brilliant, gorgeous, handsome, talented, and fabulous? ... Actually, who are you not to be?" As a single mother and technology consultant for many years, Sophia was often traveling and cherished time at home with her three children, her *Duckies,* dissecting the wonders of Life. While living in Tallahassee, on a Tuesday night, you may have found her sharing on the open mic at Black on Black Rhyme poetry held at Nefetari's Fine Cuisine or doing the two-step to southern soul music at the old Grenadier Shriners Club. Atlanta served as a "metaphysical Mecca" for Sophia and the landscape for the next phases of her spiritual, and sexual, growth, exploration, and development. In 2015, Sophia performed at Sex Down South's *Eroticology* event which motivated her to produce a chapbook of her poems entitled, *The Rebirth Fulfilled*, which highlighted a significant part of her journey of awakening and rebirth and the emergence of her true Badass Self.

Contact her at *amazenbydesign@gmail.com* for more information, to order her new book, request her for poetry or speaking events, or just to say "Hi."

THANK YOU FOR READING!

LOVE NOTES FROM, SOPHIA

Made in Lawrenceville, GA
29 August 2022

Made in the USA
Columbia, SC
19 April 2023

4fcf871f-e009-44d7-b605-4a0ee6cf4473R01